A scene from the Manhattan Theatre Club production of "Three Viewings." Set design by James Noone.

Photo by Joan Marcus

THREE VIEWINGS

BY JEFFREY HATCHER

★

DRAMATISTS
PLAY SERVICE
INC.

★

SPECIAL NOTE

SPECIAL NOTE ON SONGS AND RECORDINGS

For
P.E.H. and C.V.H.

THREE VIEWINGS was produced by Manhattan Theatre Club (Lynne Meadow, Artistic Director; Barry Grove, Managing Director), in New York City, on March 14, 1995. It was directed by Mary B. Robinson; the set design was by James Noone; the costume design was by Michael Krass; the lighting design was by Pat Dignan; the sound design was by Bruce Ellman and the production stage manager was Tom Aberger. The cast was as follows:

EMIL .... Buck Henry
MAC .... Margaret Whitton
VIRGINIA .... Penny Fuller

THREE VIEWINGS was first developed by Illusion Theater (Michael Robins and Bonnie Morris, Producing Directors), in Minneapolis, Minnesota, in September, 1994. It was directed by Kent Stephens; the lighting design was by Michael Tallman; the sound design was by Nancy Dahl and the stage manager was Joyce A.C. Lehmann. The cast was as follows:

EMIL .... Wayne Evenson
MAC .... Mary McDevitt
VIRGINIA .... Barbara Kingsley

CONTENTS

AUTHOR'S NOTES

THREE VIEWINGS consists of three connected monologues for three actors. The running time is 85-90 minutes. There is no intermission. TELL-TALE runs 25 minutes. THE THIEF OF TEARS runs 26-27 minutes. THIRTEEN THINGS ABOUT ED CARPOLOTTI runs 31-32 minutes. The three actors are never onstage together until the curtain call.

DESIGN — It is possible to perform the play on an almost bare stage. There should be no attempt to duplicate a funeral home in minute detail, nor should a grim "death theme" be emphasized. For example, there should *never* be a coffin onstage.

For the New York production at Manhattan Theatre Club, James Noone designed a simple, elegant, carpeted space with one small sofa, an end table, and, upstage, three recessed bays to house floral arrangements. The three bays revolved between pieces, so that a different set of floral arrangements was displayed for each monologue.

TELL-TALE had flowers in deep reds and purples; THE THIEF OF TEARS had white poinsettias; and THIRTEEN THINGS ABOUT ED CARPOLOTTI had flowers in yellows and golds. It was a very effective use of color.

Lighting effects should be used sparingly. TELL-TALE has precise blackouts noted in the script. THE THIEF OF TEARS allows for some light shifts in time and mood. THIRTEEN THINGS ABOUT ED CARPOLOTTI should utilize the least number and least obtrusive of light changes: no blackouts, slow-fades, etc., although a gradual and perhaps imperceptible series of changes could emphasize Virginia's growing fear and isolation until her situation changes at the end.

As for sound, there are no "effects," but there should be music in the brief (seconds) blackouts between each monologue, as the actors move off and onstage. Avoid using low-energy, funereal organ music or other "serious" pieces. Pop and swing come to mind. Frank Sinatra. Rosemary Clooney. Dean Martin and Bobby Darrin. The world of the play is closest to the songs and singers of the 1930s–1950s. Gershwin. Porter. Berlin. Kern. Rodgers and Hart.*

STAGING AND MOVEMENT — Buck Henry used the sofa twice in TELL-TALE, but it isn't necessary for Emil to ever sit. Margaret Whitton played Mac and used the sofa a bit more as her character set different scenes. As Virginia, Penny Fuller sat on the sofa and never rose. This is right. Virginia should *never* stand during her monologue.

ONE TEXT NOTE — In THIRTEEN THINGS ABOUT ED CARPOLOTTIE, the date "February 22, 1955" is written on page 61. If the actress playing the role of Virginia prefers, this date can be changed to 1945.

CHARACTERS — These are dramatic monologues. They are also *theatrical* monologues. In each play, the character speaks *directly* to the audience. There is no unseen, onstage intermediary — like a priest, a psychiatrist, or God. The characters are story-tellers, speaking to the paying customers in the dark — in the present tense, with intimacy, humor, and candor.

In TELL-TALE Emil should embody both the buoyancy and the fear of a timid man in the thrall of a great love. We

* See Special Note on Songs and Recordings on copyright page.

should be able to see and hear his passion overflow his buttoned-down persona.

In THE THIEF OF TEARS it is important that Mac exhibit the wit, edge, and quicksilver nature of a smart, funny woman who is trying to contain a horrible secret.

In THIRTEEN THINGS ABOUT ED CARPOLOTTI Virginia should not display her pain or sadness too early — not until deep into the piece at about the time she receives the blackmail threat under her door. At the beginning she is cheerful, funny, and chatty — even (especially) when talking about the circumstances of her husband's death. Obviously, this is a protective mechanism, and it is an essential part of her character. Occasionally this mechanism breaks down for a few seconds ("Where did I meet my husband?"), but she always revs back a moment later. Deeper into the play, as the bad news mounts, the mechanism wavers and finally collapses into bewilderment, panic and despair (the sequence that begins "George Erskine was embezzling from his own glass factory."), but even as her predicament grows more desperate, it is important that she doesn't slow down into her pain. Drive, speed and energy are vital to the piece. Virginia should never be played for pathos or sentimentality or "beautiful suffering." And, yes, she must smoke at the end.

In general, I'm convinced that productions of THREE VIEWINGS should avoid any attempt to overplay the themes of death, loss, and despair, which can lead to a lugubrious and humorless evening. True, each of the three pieces contains passages that must be played with raw emotion and without humor, but audiences bring their own experience of death and loss to the theater, and we don't need to hit them over the head with what they already know.

THREE VIEWINGS

TELL-TALE

A Monologue

CHARACTER

EMIL — A middle-aged man in a conservative suit.

TIME

Now.

PLACE

A funeral parlor in a small mid-western town.

TELL-TALE

A man, Emil, stands downstage in the light. Middle-aged. A conservative charcoal suit and dark tie. His jacket is buttoned.

Behind him are three floral arrangements with flowers in deep reds and purples.

Emil stares out front, slightly off to the side.

EMIL.   *(Lightly — a hushed chant.)*

    I love you.

    I love you.

    I love you.

    I love you.

    I love you.

    I love you.

    I love you.

    I love you.

    I love yo —

(He abruptly snaps his face forward.)

    She-almost-saw-me! *(A moment to steal a glance back at "her."*

Beat. He breathes a sigh of relief.)

Wheww! That was a close one. Real heart-stopper. The beat coming out of my shirt like a bomb about to explode. *Bump*-bum! *Bump*-bum! *Bump*-bum! *(He looks off to the side again.)*

This is all getting much more difficult. *(Back to front.)*

I started with just one.

"I love you."

Very quiet, very small. But audible.

"I love you."

Said to the back of her head as she moved through the room. Holding hands. Smiling. Brushing back a tear. If she turns around in the middle of "I love you," I thought, she'll catch me. She'll catch me and she'll hear, and she'll see, and she'll know. She'll catch me, and I'll be happy to be caught. But one "I love you" wasn't really enough. One "I love you" was too ... subtle. So I advanced to two.

"I love you.

I love you."

Still she didn't turn in time. I went to three.

"I love you.

I love you.

I love you."

Nothing. Now I'm up to *nine*. And this is the first time she's almost seen me say it. What would I have done if she had? It's been nine times since the first, at Carl Grunwald's funeral. Tessie in a red jacket — somewhat inappropriate, admittedly, but it stands out and that's the point — in a red jacket moving through the room, looking for her flowers, handing out her card. I was standing next to the casket, doing what we funeral directors do, when it struck me. All the years I'd known her. Same town, same people, how we're always flung together. Then, suddenly, she's in my mind all the time. First thought at morning, last thought at night. I watched her, me standing next to Carl, Tessie giving her real estate card to Ruth Grunwald. Tessie never presses her card; they always ask, she doesn't push; but they do go home with her card every time. I looked at her in her red jacket and her black hair and her blue eyes and white skin and said:

"I love you."

Even Carl could have heard me. But Tessie didn't. Tessie came up to me.

"Carl looks good," she murmured.

"Thanks. He'd lost a lot of weight in the hospital. Six weeks. I think we brought him back to snuff."

Tessie smiles. Margaret-Mary Walsh approaches the casket, and we turn, Tessie and I turn to face Margaret-Mary, together, at the casket, both of us greeting her. Like a couple. The most natural thing in the world. *(He stares off at "her.")*

It's been nine times now. Next time I'll have to go up to ten. *(Blackout. Lights come up. Emil faces out front.)*

Nettie James died yesterday. She was 103. Been on the verge of death for twenty-eight years. Coal money. Very rich. Terrible woman. The Herald-Star made up a headline for her obituary that read "Nettie James FINALLY Dies. Civic And Social Leader Succumbs After A Lifetime Of Condescension And

Bullying." They didn't print it. It's a big affair. Private service. I got Tessie in. Not that the James family is going to sell the house on Norton Place let alone use Tessie's real estate company, but it's good for Tessie to be seen, and I got her on the list. She's in the visitation room. Nettie James looks very small in her casket. She was tissue paper and cobwebs these last few … decades. I'm up to 12.

I love you.

I love you.

I love you.

I love you.

I love you.

I love you.

I love you.

I love you.

She never turns. Admittedly, I tend to start my chant when she's deep in conversation with someone — Margaret-Mary Walsh, Bob O'Klock, Art Wise — so there's little *chance* of her suddenly turning to look at *me*. Wouldn't it be wonderful if she suddenly turned to look at me? What if I could catch her eyes, suddenly turning to look at me? A man can always feel a woman's irises clicking in her head when she turns to steal a glance at him. He can feel it in his peripheral vision. A little blue and white whip — at you and back. Look back at her, and the blue whips away. If I could feel that … then I'd know. There's nothing more obvious in life than one person looking longingly at another — unless it's a person desperately trying *not* to look at all.

I love you.

I love you.

I love you.

I love you.

I hate her name. Tessie. Not Teresa, not Tess — Tessie. She used to be married. Marvin Vankirk. He's at Wintersville High, teaches math. "Expectations plus Marvin equals reality." They're still friendly. Marvin re-married. Estelle Calabria. Tessie got her real estate license after the divorce. Got the idea when Johnny Criss and Joe Bethel and Dale Featheringham and the rest of the ten percenters all came to her mother's funeral. Now Tessie's part of the pack. But she's different. Maybe I just *think* she's different. *(Beat. He thinks.)*

No, she's different.

I love you.

I love you.

We go into the service. The Reverend Dr. James A. Zimbro, III, officiating. I won't say Jim Zimbro's an *unimaginative* minister, but he *is* known in the trade as "The Rev. Dr. *INSERT DECEASED'S NAME HERE*." He begins.

"The love that lasts...."

My mind withdraws to other places. It's a depressed real estate market. That's why Criss, Bethel, the whole bunch swoop down so. It's harder for Tessie, but she's talented and she has more than promise. I know. The way she can describe a house.... I've almost bought four myself. She's on commission, and it's getting tight. A slow season. She tells me about wanting to travel, to get away. Mexico. The Berkshires. Spain. I tell her how difficult it is for *me* to get away:

"No slow season."

She laughs. *Her laugh.* Her smile. "Her flashing eyes, her floating hair."

She has not had an easy life. Father was an alcoholic — mother spent twelve years dying in the state hospital — the divorce. And she wears a pacemaker, Tessie — something congenital — to regulate her heart.

I love you.

I love you.

I love you.

I have to help her. I will find a way to help her. *(Blackout. Lights come up.)*

I have started to give Tessie advance word of imminent deaths. Sometimes I get a warning. Hospital. Police. "A friend in power." Last week Bill Goodpastor tells me his wife Marge has a brain tumor, Bill thinks she may not last the week. Marge looked so old last time she came here. And Bill, Bill still looks like Paul Newman on sheep-gland injections. Marge is dying, the house is too big, Bill told me, I told Tessie. Unethical? Maybe. It's a slippery slope, but passion is a bracing lubricant.

I love you

I love you

I love you

I'm up to seventeen now. I'm starting to think she *knows* I'm saying it, and that's why she *doesn't* turn. I have considered driving past her house at night. The light in the window, the nose pressed against the pane. But I have restrained myself. That way leads to madness, the padded cell, the perch in the book depository window. I am not like that. Why don't I just tell her? What's the worst that could happen? Mockery. Humiliation. A howl of derision followed by twenty years of averted glances. There should be a kind of safety net for these moments. A magic "shroud" you could use. You go up to the woman, you say:

"I've been meaning to tell you: I love you."

If she says,

"I love you, too,"

great, fantastic, everybody goes to the prom. If she gets red in the face, takes your hand, and says:

"That's *so* flattering, you're *such* a *friend*,"

then you say,

"Excuse me, but I have to lower the magic shroud now."

And she forgets everything said to her in the last thirty seconds.

"You're such a friend."

A knife in the heart. Anyway, Marge Goodpastor died yesterday. Bill called from his Jaguar. Tessie came early to the visitation — I wanted to introduce her to Bill before the rush and the cremation. I am making this vow: If my "I love you" gambit does not prove fruitful, I will take drastic action. I will tell her my true feelings before the year is out. Tomorrow is Thanksgiving. Jim Zimbro is talking about "the love that lasts." I have 35 days. *(Lights fade. Lights come up. Smiles.)*

19

Tessie said "I hate you" today, and I think there's hope! At The Green Mill. We bumped into each other outside the bank, Christmas shopping. I offered lunch. She said she had to meet Bill Goodpastor to show his house.

"BUT,"

she says ... and I quote her ....

"OH — WHAT THE HELL — *LET'S* — *HAVE* — *LUNCH.*" *(Big proud grin and giggle.)*

What do you think of *that!* We were talking about these last few "referrals" I've made her. She sold three houses. Good commissions. She's breathing a little easier now, and she wanted to take *me* to lunch. I told her,

"You know, I can't keep slipping you these tips forever, we're gonna run out, I'll have to start killing them myself." *(He laughs, mock-sinister.)*

HEH-HEH-HEH. She laughed. She said,

"You're terrible, I hate you!"

And she *slapped* me! Just my lower arm, across the table, next to the coffee cup. Her fingers brushed my wrist, near my watch, skin to skin. I almost jumped. Red face. Adrenalin. Dizziness. Vertigo. Just a touch on my wrist. This has happened to me before. This *sort* of thing. It goes away. I let it run its course. Lasts a few weeks. This one is in its eleventh month. Is it painful? It hurts ... but not like hell. I'd rather have this particular pain than ... its particular absence. "Desire plus denial equals...." Well, I'm not a Catholic — so I don't know what the hell it equals. It has gone on too long though. Fury or humiliation, I will tell her by December 31st. New Year's Eve. But I wish she'd *guess* it first. I wish she'd tell *me*. Read my mind, read my lips. Maybe I'll start using code. Writing "I love you" in the floral tributes or underneath the lids of the caskets. Cryptography in the swirls of a dead person's hair. "Find the Nina." Suddenly — out of nowhere — she asks me a question.

"Do you know when you're in love?"

My heart has stopped.

"What?"

"I *said*," she says, "Do you know when you're in love."

"Oh yes."

"How?"

I'm stalling for time. I'm trying to think, but I'm on fire, my brain is swimming, the floor tilts, a descent into maelstrom. Finally, I manage — a cracked voice at the bottom of my shoes.

"You always know. Knowing isn't the point. The point is action. The point is speaking. That kind of action, that kind of courage ..."

I'm swirling in her eyes, her hair. She is smart, she is bright, she has depth and breadth and the world is lit by lightning!

"Why do you ask?" I ask.

She doesn't smile. She looks at me. Three seconds, eye to eye. One. I love you. Two. I love you. Three. I love you. I'm shouting the words in my mind, *but my lips are sealed,* surely

21

she can hear me, PLEASE, GOD, LET HER HEAR ME! She breaks her stare.

"Never mind."

She'll pay the check, I'll leave the tip. Exiting, I place my hand under her elbow. She allows it. She does not comment. Outside, she kisses me goodbye. Cheek. Another detonation to the skin. My heart is racing. She walks away. The last I see of her is a slip on a patch of ice. Then she rights herself, and turns the corner. Today is December 7. A date that will live in infamy. I have 24 more shopping days. *(Blackout. Lights come up. Tense and angry.)*

Ed Carpolotti died, and Tessie didn't come to the funeral. It was a *three day affair!* I'd left a message on her machine telling her about Ed. Just the usual. But there was no reply. A day passes. I call her again, get her machine, leave another message. No reply. Two days more, the day of the burial, December 21st, the longest day of the year. I tell Jim Zimbro:

"We should go another day, not everyone who would want to see Ed has had the chance."

Jim looks at me like I'm nuts.

"You want to *extend* it?"

"What about Art Wise," I sputter. "And Johnny Criss. And Joe Bethel and Dale Featheringham and Bill Goodpastor...."

"Bill's in Florida," says Jim. "He went down Friday. He and Tessie."

Bump-bum ... bump-bum ... bump-bum ... bump-bum ... I *slam* down the coffin lid!

"Let's get this goddamn show on the road!"

I *propel* Ed Carpolotti into the service room, the coffin cart banging into the door frame as I take the turn on two wheels! My heart is *pounding!* Had she been seeing him long? Was it *him* she was talking about at The Green Mill? Did I *miss* something? Was I *confused?* Was there a *code* she was using? Had she been saying "I LOVE YOU" TO *ME* AND I JUST WASN'T LISTENING? DOES SHE HAVE ANY INKLING AT *ALL? AM I A <u>FOOL</u>!* Blood is crashing against the rocks in my ears! *BUMP-BUM! BUMP-BUM! BUMP-BUM! Will someone not stop this ridiculous heartbeat! Surely, everyone will hear it! Surely everyone in the room can HEAR IT!!! (He has reached an explosive crescendo. He finally stops, looks out, fearing he's been caught. His voice is a hushed rasp.)*

But they do not turn, they do not hear, they do not see. I am not caught. Afterwards, Margaret-Mary Walsh takes me aside and tells me she has never been so moved by a service. The woman has always been good and kind, one of my "regulars." So I do not hit her. *(Blackout. Lights come up.)*

I was on a bus once in a large city and sitting next to me was a young man. Across from the man was a beautiful woman. They were making eye contact. Look at him, look away — look at her, look away. The tension was enormous. We all got off at the same stop, and as we stepped onto the sidewalk, the young man approached the woman and said,

"I noticed you on the bus."

What courage that man had! What faith and daring! He had seen another face on this planet and thought to himself,

"*I* will not slink into the night regretting the lost opportunities, the might-have-beens. *I* will not die a thousand coward's deaths! I will gather every drop of strength I have! This will change my life!"

"I NOTICED YOU ON THE BUS!"

And the woman said, "So?" and walked away.

He will always be my hero. *(Beat.)*

The hospital called me at eleven twenty two. An accident on the drive from the airport. Icy roads after Christmas, a slippery slope, a Jaguar over the hill. Bill Goodpastor is dead. So is his passenger. *(Pause.)*

As Tessie's family is gone … Marvin Vankirk will make the funeral arrangements. Marvin calls me after midnight. Will I take care of her personally? Not one of the assistants, or pop who still comes in occasionally. Me.

"You were such a friend of Terri's."

Terri. Huh.

They bring her in the next afternoon. It's the law, when there has been no previous illness or attending physician at the time of death, to conduct an autopsy on a body. Which means … that … certain surgical procedures have already been completed. I ask pop to help me in the prep room. I don't want to be alone. He hobbles down, his cane, his shake. I notice her hair. Gray at the roots. Was she letting it grow out? Or did she just not have the chance to color it? I attach the machine, I prepare the instruments — needles, tubes. Her partial plate out, I smooth the crows feet around her eyes. I do ... what we do ... to her eyes, her lips. What we do is ... we seal them. *(Pause.)* The funeral is crowded. Johnny Criss is there and Joe Bethel and Dale Featheringham. And Reverend Zimbro, Mr. Fill in the Blank. Zimbro asks Marvin if there is anything he should add to the service. I open my mouth:

"Say something about Mexico, the Berkshires and Spain."

I've spoken too loudly. Heads have turned. Across the room I see my wife — *(He looks out front.)* Oh yes. Marvin tells us it was Terri...'s wish to be cremated.

"Her ashes will be scattered over Mexico," says Marvin, solemnly ... whenever Marvin and Estelle save up the money to have a "real vacation." We do the final viewing. The final service. The casket is closed. And by three o'clock that afternoon, Teresa is gone. Little known facts. Some things don't burn in a crematorium. Diamonds. Some metals. Heavier bones. Some things you *can't* burn. Like pace-makers. The heat makes them explode. You can damage the inside of the chamber. So it's important to remove them before you ... set fire to the body. *(He holds up a small transistor-sized object.)*

I found this in the preparation room. I really should have given it back to ... someone else. *(He holds it up to his ear.)*

It keeps on ticking. Tonight is New Year's Eve. My wife is upstairs in bed early, and there aren't any customers in the viewing rooms. For the first time in memory ... we are entirely empty. *(He holds the pacemaker and looks off at "her.")*

Turn around. Turn around. Look at me, sweetie. Please look at me this time. I'll say it again. I'll say it a thousand times until you turn around and catch me. I love you — one I love you — two … *(Lights fade to black.)*

THE END

THE THIEF OF TEARS

A Monologue

CHARACTER

Mac, a woman in her 30s or 40s dressed in black and wearing many sparkling rings.

TIME

Now.

PLACE

A funeral parlor in a small mid-western town.

THE THIEF OF TEARS

Lights up on Mac, an attractive woman between the ages of 35 and 45. Mac wears black. Lots of sparkling rings on her fingers. Behind her are three floral arrangements — white poinsettias.

MAC.   I've been stealing jewelry off corpses for years, Grandma'll be a fuckin' cinch. *(Beat.)*

Let me go back. The phone call of the dead always comes between midnight and one A.M. Before midnight, the call could be anyone for any reason. After one, it's a wrong number dialed in Spain. But if the call comes in *between* midnight and one, the news is a Houseboat on the River Styx and no mistake, Charlie. When I get back to my apartment from the Viper Room, the electronic guy on the answering machine says 12:48. It's Donald's voice.

"Heigh-ho, Mac, father this end. We're at the Philadelphia house. Call us collect ASAP. Hope A-OK your end. Ten-four."

My father never says goodbye. He says, "Ten-four" or "A-OK." It's a superstition. If he says "goodbye" he knows he'll die soon in a fiery plane crash. I look at the clock near the bed. Four thirty-six A.M. If it's four thirty in Los Angeles that means it's seven thirty in America. They'll be up now in Philadelphia — which is unfortunate because it means my call will not wake them. I pour a drink — vodka — as it's morning.

And I dial. Donald picks up.

"It's Nettie," he says. "She died last night. At Norton Place. We're driving down. Are you able to get a flight to Pittsburgh? Do you need anything?"

"Yes," I say, "I can get a flight out. And no, I don't need anything." ("Anything," in our family, means money.)

"Roger, then," says Donald. "Over and out."

We hang up. She's dead. My grandmother, Nettie James is dead. This is my moment. My destiny has called me. I pour another vodka and rifle through a shoebox in the closet to find the cracked black-and-white photograph I know is there. This photo goes back *with* me. I look at the figure passed out on the bed. Someone in black named Raymond or Charlotte or ... Lassie. That *won't* go back with me. I should call USAIR to see if I can get a flight at nine. But first I look in my wallet. A twenty and three ones. The bank account is overdrawn, and all my plastic is strictly Dead Zone. I need money for a plane ticket and a rental car and three days in the worst place on earth. I will have to go to work! The L.A. Times is delivered early, so I go for the door and head straight to Section D. – Rosalind Marquardt. 83. Tarzana. *(Thinks.)*

No. – Elizabeth Quilty. 69. West Hollywood. Nup. – Miriam Cass. 86. *Beverly Hills.* Miriam Cass. Survived by her husband, Maurice. Viewing at nine. So I'll get a later flight. By nine o'clock I'm at the funeral home on Sunset Boulevard, my bags in the back of the taxi I've asked to wait. I dawdle until a crowd has formed. A field of blue hair and blue stoles. Maurice must be the old blind guy in the 1964 Savile Row suit.

I pay my respects to Maurice, my condolences, how I met Miriam — *MeMee, yes* — on the trip to, to — *Ceylon, exactly*! How MeMee spoke of Maurice — yes, *while* he was sick in their stateroom. I'll just say goodbye. And then there I am in the line, two people away from the — *(Snaps fingers.)*

Score — *open casket!* I inhale. Swallow. Somehow in this business, it's always the first time. I close my eyes, bite my lips, and the tears well up. I bend over to kiss Miriam goodbye, noting that she is absolutely *encrusted*. Two pecks on the corpse — on either side of the face, in the continental manner. When I pull back, I have my mouth firmly shut — a supreme effort not to lose control of my emotions. Once I'm in the cab I open my mouth and take out the earrings. Ladies and gentlemen, Jack Rubies. My fence will give me three thousand for them, which is enough for an open-end return ticket, a good rental car, and plenty of scratch until I get mine from Nettie James! *(Pause.)*

Four hours later, on the plane over the tundra, a glass of champagne stapled to my palm. Thomas Wolfe once wrote: "You can't go home again." *(Beat.)*

Thomas Wolfe was a putz, of *course* you can go home again, they *make* you go home, *all the time* — <u>*endlessly*</u>! But this time is different. I'm going to *get* something from *this* trip. High over Ohio, I close my eyes and imagine I'm on "The Charlie Rose Show." The dark background, the Persian carpet, the good wood. Jodie Foster has just left, and Gore Vidal is in the wings. Charlie turns his cleft to me.

"How'd ya' get your *start* in — well — I guess we'd *have* to call it — heck ... *corpse-robbing*, right?"

"Right you are, Charlie. *Weel*, it was like this, you big, dumb handsome guy they make read books: I had just moved from Stockbridge to L.A., I was broke, not acting. A friend of mine died, a bad death. I hadn't been to a funeral in a long time, and they'd put me in charge of accessorizing him for the viewing, but his wrists were so small, his watch wouldn't fit, so I put it in my purse for later. It wasn't until three days after the funeral that I realized I still had the watch. I was gonna give it back ... but it was a Rolex in a rough week. And anyway give it back to whom? So I rationalized keeping the watch ... then selling it ... then finding ways to do it again. It's kept me in high five figures for eight years now. Never caught, knock on cherry wood or knotty pine. I even know some other people in the business now. We recognize each other at funerals. Tricks of the trade stuff: who's using lubricant, pliers, wire cutters. I saw a chick with a magnet once, she was a fuckin' trip, man. Some jobs are dicier than others, of course. I got a gold tooth once. Don't ask."

"But gosh," says Mr. Rose, "is there anything you *won't* steal?"

"Sure. A wedding ring. A friendship ring. A decoder ring. There are limits."

"But why do you do it? What do you want?"

"Want? The touch of something that has touched another. Bring on Gore Vidal, pal. Ask *him* what *he* wants."

At Pittsburgh I rent a BMW, and an hour out of the airport — past steel mills, past strip mines, past the same farm for fifty miles — I arrive over the river and through the woods to grandmother's funeral. Inside the parlor, the first viewing has begun. My parents, Donald and Dorothy stand at the first position nearest the head of the casket, receiving the dukes and barons of the town. In the far corner sits my mother's sister, Aunt Teeta, pleasant, smiling, sweet, an idiot. At the rear near the exit is her only son Gerald and my brother, St. David, the Perfect. I look out on a jungle of white poinsettias (it's gotten out that Nettie *loved* white poinsettias). It looks like we're burying her on the set of *Dr. Zhivago*. I squint below a snowy plant and there I see one lone figure. It's Josephine, Nettie's housekeeper on Norton Place. She was my grandmother's H.R. Haldeman.

"You know me, Josephine?"

She nods.

"You remember me, Josephine?"

She does.

"You're the bi-polar, bi-sexual drug addict."

Donald and Dorothy give an imperceptible glance in my direction. It's actually a glare. It wouldn't look like a glare to anyone else, but to a James, it's a glare. Kind of like how only dogs can hear certain sounds. My brother David has suddenly sidled up to me. I can smell the Pepto Bismol on his breath.

"After the viewing, Mother and Father want to have a talk with us."

Then David slips back to his post near the flowers from something called the First Church of the Charismatic Assumption. I can sense tension in the room. They're all acting — well — they're acting as if someone has *died*. Nettie James was 103 years old. This funeral has been in rehearsal so long it's had replacement casts. But somehow the relaxed jocularity one associates with the death of a very old, very demanding, very rich harridan is entirely absent. I mouth to Josephine:

"What's going on?"

She smiles.

"There's a new will."

Minutes later the family is gathered in a spare viewing parlor where my father, Donald, is interrogating a young local attorney named Danny Spahr about how "it" could have happened.

"Five-point-two million dollars left to the First Church of the Charismatic Assumption? The Norton Place house and the Lake Cottage left to Charismatic Alternative Families, Inc.? My wife's mother left the entire family fortune to a bunch of crazed holy-roller devil-worshippers?"

Danny Spahr shrugs.

"I warned you to disconnect her Cable TV."

The will has been read. The money is gone. This they will have to get used to. But I have not come for money. I have come for something else. Let me go back. In the black-and-white photograph I've brought with me from L.A. a beautifully-coiffed woman in her sixties holds the hand of an equally beautifully-coiffed five-year-old girl with red eyes from crying, only you can't see the red in black and white, but you can see the tears. It's 1963, and I'm *not* going to go to the beauty parlor. I'm screaming in the back of the big blue Packard, and my grandmother has decided to calm me down by taking me into the big department store, The Hub. She holds my hand, and when we enter, hundreds of shop clerks rush to greet us, bending, grovelling, rubbing their hands. Mrs. Bordenkirker from the shoe department, Miss Carver from the dress department, Morton Lincoff from jewelry. They give her presents. Something especially important seems to come from Morton Lincoff. Something wrapped in a box. Nettie turns to me and says,

"You see? If you're nice to people, they'll give you things. Tell you what: you be a good girl today when you get your hair done, and Nettie'll *give* you what's in this box."

And she opens it. Inside is a beautiful tear-shaped ring. It seems to sparkle with every jewel in the planet. I've never seen such color, so many facets, such light. I will do *anything* to get this ring. So I *am* a good girl, and I *do* calm down, and I *get* my hair done. And when it's all over, and we're back at Norton Place, and Josephine is about to take our picture, I ask my grandmother,

"So where's my present?"

And Nettie says —

"Oh, that was just something I *said.* You can't always get what you *want.*"

And the ring goes on <u>her</u> finger.

The family returns to the parlor where the second viewing has begun. There's a crowd around the casket so I decide to take a stroll through the competing parlors. I peer around, casing the joint, when a little old woman who seems to *live* at the funeral home — she has her own *chair* — comes up to me through the white forest. Her name is Margaret Mary Walsh and she remembers me since I was, I dunno, an *embryo*, sperm with eyelashes. We trade inane nonsense for a while. I sound like a cake-mix lobotomy. Finally she remembers the missing piece in my puzzle:

"And how is your husband and family?"

Imperceptibly, I can feel David flinch, Teeta wince, Donald and Dorothy blush. But I am fine. I tell Margaret Mary Walsh:

"I'm not married anymore. My husband never fixed the kitchen door."

This seems to satisfy her. The crowd around the coffin has gone on a coffee break, so I make a bee-line for the casket. I peer in at my grandmother. A voice nearby murmurs:

"She looks good."

I nod. (She looks like Stalin.) Her hands are folded, touching, one over the other. She always wore the dinner ring on her right hand, aaannnd ... that's the hand I cannot see. It's covered by the other one. My fingers itch to pick it up, turn it over ... but I keep my cool.

"Just looking."

How am I going to find out if she's wearing that ring? Suddenly, Donald is at my side:

"Mac, we have a problem. Nettie's new will left instructions specifying certain pieces of jewelry she wanted to be buried with. The funeral home won't take responsibility for the pieces overnight. Their policy is to have the family do the *physical removal* from the body and keep the jewels at home until morning. Now, your mother is in no state to do it, nor is Aunt Teeta. Nor me. Nor your brother, he can't touch dead people."

(David is a surgeon, o.k.?)

"We'd like *you* to do it, Mac." *(Beat.)*

"Oh. I *couldn't.*"

"MAC: Your mother and I didn't stop you from going to Los Angeles when you *should* have stayed in the hospital in Stockbridge. We didn't even stop you when you changed your first name from Jane to ... McTeague. This is a family service we are requesting. One we expect to be performed. Unless you feel you are ... *incapable.*"

I look at my parents. "All *right*," I say, "Sure. I've been stealing jewelry off corpses for years, Grandma'll be a fuckin' cinch." *(She looks at the audience as if to say "This is where you came in.")*

I go to my grandmother. I remove the jewelry. I try to make it all look like it takes longer than it does. Then I very deftly *flip* her left hand off her right. There is *no* tear-shaped dinner ring. Her fingers are bare. I pat her down like a cop at the airport. It's not there. Nothing. In a daze, I give the other pieces to Donald. Then I take my rented BMW, drive to a place called The Green Mill and get drunk with a feed salesman named Duane who can't get his wedding ring off fast enough, an action that makes me so sad and depressed I say horrible things about feed salesmen and go back to Norton Place very alone. I'm in the pink room of my grandmother's home, in the pink bed that's been mine since I was a child. In the darkness, I dream of Jack in the night. Jack in our house in Stockbridge, holding hands with Paul and Lainie at his side.

"Why can't you love the littlest things," he says. "The things you can hold in your hand. What do you *want* from this world?" "There are so many things you can't get or hold on to. Like color, and facets, and light."

And then — in the dream — Jack takes my hand, places three rings on my fingers ... and says:

"Is that why you tried to kill yourself?" *(Pause.)*

"Yes. I left our bed and I went into the garage, and I sat in the car in the cold, cold night and turned on the ignition. I *tried.* Didn't work out the way I'd planned." *(Pause.)*

The next morning ... I call the airport to get the soonest possible flight back to L.A. My bags are in the BMW outside the funeral home. *Inside* ... I'm at my post for the third and *final* viewing ... when out of the field of poinsettias, I notice a tiny bald man deep in conversation with Josephine and Margaret Mary Walsh. They're whispering together. They look in my direction, and the bent, hobbled old gnome approaches. It's *Morton Lincoff!* Morton Lincoff from The Hub! He's ancient now — like Yoda. And much to my surprise because what are the chances? — he says to me:

"Where is that husband and those two kids?"

My words come out as ever.

"I am not married now. My husband never fixed the kitchen door."

I try to walk away. But Morton Lincoff is persistent.

"You know, I remember you coming into the store with your grandmother — must have been thirty years ago — the day you were going to get your first hair done. Your grandmother had come in to pick up a ring your grandfather had me design. A dinner ring. Beautiful thing. The one she's wearing right now."

I am Morton Lincoff's oxygen, my face so close to his.

"You mean the, the *tear*-shaped ring?"

"Yes!" he beams. "Beautiful work from a talented wholesale genius I had in Hackensack, only came to town twice, three times a year. Your grandmother had sent it in to be cleaned before she died. I just give it back to Mister Funeral. Your grandmother, she wanted she should be buried with it, and who are we to argue with the dead?"

It's there. It's *there*. Why shouldn't I take it? It was, by rights — it was by rights ... *mine*. And I need — I *want* — The service is about to begin. The family is to pay its last tributes. One by one. As they do, I go to the powder room, so that when I return, I will be the last. This is an affront to protocol, of course, but it's the best method. It's worked for me a billion times, it'll work for me again. Out of the bathroom, I sustain the glares, but I am resolute. No one dare stop the emotional grand-daughter from her final embrace. I approach the subject. My grandmother. My mother's mother. The source of my being. Cold and dusted pink and blue. I look down. The ring is there. The Eagle has landed. I grip the side of the casket. I lean my face to hers. I kiss her cheek — and place my hand upon her hand. Her ring is harder to remove than I had hoped, as if the finger's swelled. I pull. Nothing. I twist. Nothing. I do not want to break her finger. It is an occupational hazard, and I don't want my grandmother to be my first "snapper." And then I look down. Because Nettie's eyes — my grandmother's eyes — are wide open and watching me.

"Grandma?"

"Hello, Jane. Going to steal my ring?"

Uh ... maybe.

"Sweet Janie. Why have you been lying to my old friends about that family of yours?"

Her hand has mine gripped in a lock so strong, so tight, my fingers will break!!

"You've been lying, Jane. I won't let go 'til you tell Grandma where that husband of yours is and my two great-grandchildren."

I am pulling away from her now, but her hand has my wrist, now my elbow, now pulling me deep towards her face!

"Tell me the truth, Janie. Why have you been lying? Where is that husband of yours and my great-grandchildren?"

I am running a cold sweat, I look for my family — my *family!* — and there's no one in the room!

"Where is your family. Where is your family! *Where is your family!*" I shout out.

My husband never fixed the kitchen door! And after I fell asleep in the garage, I finally woke up at the hospital in Stockbridge and I asked where is my husband, where is my daughter, where is my son ... they explained to me ... that because the kitchen was attached to the garage, and because the kitchen door had never been fixed, the lock had opened, and the door had opened, and the air from the garage had drifted into the house and into the bedrooms and my family — my husband, my children, my littlest things ... it had killed my family ... while I slept.

Let me go back. Let me go back! *Let me go back!*

And the ring comes off! Someone touches my shoulder. It's time to close the casket. At the graveside, they place the coffin deep in the ground next to my grandfather's old headstone. The earth begins to hit the top of the casing with the sound that is unmistakably it. I am listening to the minister talk about the gift of the homemaker, the ring clasped tight in my hand. *(Beat.)*

I did not die the day I tried to kill myself. They buried my family before I had a chance to touch them, hold their hands one more time. Jack's wedding ring. Lainie's friendship ring. Paul's decoder ring. All deep in the ground before I woke up. But I am alive, and my grandmother's ring is cold to my touch. It is not what I want or need. At long last, the minister is finished. My mother steps forward and throws in a clump of dirt. Then Aunt Teeta. Then Donald and David and Gerald. Finally, there is me. I go to the hole cut out of the planet. I gather the dirt. And I let it fall. The clump of a clod of earth — the sprinkle of grain and rock — the rain of dust. And the silver note as the ring bounces off the lid and disappears deep into the soil. Forever. *(Pause. Mac kneels and begins to remove her rings, until by the end of the next speech, she looks like a mourner from the old country, dressed in black.)*

In Stockbridge, Massachusetts, where I lived for years, there is a place where my other family is buried. I have not yet visited them. But I know the way there. In the darkness, I pray for the touch of a hand that has known my touch too. The call of the dead is not strange in the night. No one can steal anything from my family — ever again. Tears freeze in the cold. When they hit the stone they break into a shattering of colors and facets and light. I gather them close to me, and I am warm like a thief in the night. *(Slow fade end of play.)*

THIRTEEN THINGS
ABOUT ED CARPOLOTTI

A Monologue

CHARACTER

VIRGINIA — A woman in her late 50s or 60s with a cigarette and lighter.

TIME

Now.

PLACE

A funeral parlor in a small mid-western town.

THIRTEEN THINGS
ABOUT ED CARPOLOTTI

Lights up on a woman, Virginia. In her late 50s or 60s, a pleasant suburban matron in expensive, tailored black. Virginia sits on a small sofa or love seat. A gold-headed cane leans against the love seat. A purse sits to her side. Next to her purse, unobtrusive, is a small manila envelope. Virginia holds an unlit cigarette in one hand, a lighter in the other. Behind her are three floral arrangements in yellows and golds. Virginia begins speaking immediately as the lights bump up.

VIRGINIA.   *(Upbeat and energetic.)* Ed always said I couldn't keep my mouth shut. Well, he didn't *always* say it. I think he said it *once*. He was never a talker. Even *before* we were married. He'd clam up at dinners, parties. He knew I hated him being so quiet. I'd say to him!

"Ed, at least *look* like you're talking to me!"

So he tried. Whenever he didn't have anything to say, he'd turn to me and start to mutter:

"Mary had a little lamb," he'd say.

And I'd come back, "His fleece was white as snow."

"And everywhere that Mary went."

You get the idea. People thought we had quite a rapport! *Well.* Ed gave up smoking four months before he died. When he had his first heart attack, he'd been on "the patch" since early September. Even while he was in the hospital, before the second one hit him and all the "funny" business started to happen, Ed joked he was "down to two and a half patches a day." I told him the biggest change it made was in our sex life. It's just not romantic to turn to the person next to you after it's all over and offer her a small package to stick on her ribcage. He still had one on him pumping away the night he died. That was in Pittsburgh. We'd moved Ed to Allegheny General when things started to go hay-wire. St. Joseph's here in town isn't equipped for that kind of thing — by which I mean decent hospital care when your life depends on it. We moved Ed on Thanksgiving morning, during the broadcast of the Macy's Parade. Debbie made all the arrangements. By the time the ambulance got him up there his watch and one of his rings had been stolen They even got his gold medic-alert necklace. We should have taken them off. Debbie said she'd even thought about it but felt creepy wrestling her father's jewelry off before they carted him away. Something about it being *"too Dickensian for words." (She looks out front.)*

I never know what Debbie's talking about. Ed gave up smoking on Labor Day, he had his first heart attack on Halloween, his second on Thanksgiving, and he died just before Christmas. Well, he loved holidays. When we brought him back to the funeral home, the undertaker's assistant asked us if there was anything else he could do to make Ed look more natural?

"Give 'im a goddamn cigarette."

Natural. He's dead wearing bifocals and a hairpiece, what's going to help the illusion of reality here? Debbie picked out the suit and tie. The pocket hankie. The cuff-links shaped like bulldozers. The hair-piece. He had a lot of them in the bathroom. All of his hair on these little white heads. You could watch Ed age on those heads. After the funeral, Debbie told me she'd slipped a pack of Camels into her father's pocket before they closed the casket —

"— sort of as a symbol, like the Egyptians or the Vikings taking a talisman into the great beyond." *(She looks out again.)*

I never know what she's talking about. Debbie's back home in Wisconsin now — with her second husband, the assistant provost, and the twins — and her unfinished novel ... about a woman in Wisconsin with her second husband, the assistant provost, and her twins. I thought about calling her after the funeral when things started to happen, but she's listening to Prozac and I don't want to interrupt. I can't remember where or when I met Ed. Tootie Vaughn would remember. Tootie's my best galfriend, and she remembers things like this, but I don't. All I remember was living at home with Mother and Daddy and then there was Ed. He'd left his dad's grocery store and was going to build highways and roads and bridges. He had no money and no prospects and Mother and Daddy did not approve. I had to sneak out of the house to see him once. Mother and Daddy thought I'd gone with Tootie to see Martin and Lewis in *My Friend Irma Goes West,* but I'd gone out to Stone Road with Ed. When I got back Tootie was in our living room with a guilty look on her face, and Daddy quizzed

me about where I'd gone. I always know when I've done something wrong. I start to sweat on my ... well, it's not polite to
say it, but ... my *collarbone*. I flush. I get red there. Nobody
can *see* it but I can *feel* it. I lied of course. Said I "had *so* gone
to the movies." Daddy said

"Prove it,"

so I made up an entire plot for *My Friend Irma Goes West*. The
next night I went to see *My Friend Irma Goes West* and was
surprised to learn just how close I'd got!

I wasn't there when he died. Debbie wasn't either. No one
was. Three A.M., a week before Christmas. The nurses said he
didn't make a sound when the aneurysm hit.

"Why didn't he cry out?" I asked. "Isn't it painful?"

"Oh, yes," they said, "but what with the dementia that set
in following the second cardiovascular infarction your
husband's responses had become neurologically inappropriate."

At the service, Margaret-Mary Walsh tells me he was lucky
to go that way. I guess. He recognized Debbie once towards
the end, but he thought we were in Las Vegas. He thought I
was his mother. One night he saw a cow in the room standing behind me.

"Yeah," I tell her, "I'd like to die in Las Vegas with my
mother and a cow too."

The funeral was.... Lots of people. Bob O'Klock from the
bank. Dino DiSperbio from Smith Trucking. Ed's brother
Frank. Funerals make me tired. Even other people's. I don't
know how the undertakers do it. They *prefer* the title "morti-
cian" but that always sounds like death with air-freshener to

me. "Undertaker" is right. They undertake what we can't bear. *(She looks off.)*

When did I meet Ed? Where did I meet my husband? *(A beat. She focuses again.)*

It was three days before I could get down to the office. The way the will's written I'm president of "Ed Carpolotti, Inc." now. *President.* Debbie asks me over the phone if my "first official act will be to recognize Cuba." *(She laughs a trill.)*

I laugh ... like I know what the hell she's talking about. Ed's secretary, Joy, showed me what our attorney said I needed to see. On paper, it looked like the construction business had been slow — Well, business had been *bad* the past year or so. But the files showed assets. We'd be fine. I said that to Joy.

"We'll be fine."

And Joy just *looked* at me. I went to see our attorney the next day. I depend on Danny Spahr, but it's hard to invest a lot of authority in the little boy who used to deliver your milk. I go down to his office at the bank building. Bob O'Klock's bank, where Ed's company did business. Bob smiles and waves at me from behind the glass doors in the lobby. *(She imitates his "call me" hand action.)*

Makes a motion with his hand that either means to give him a call ... or he wants me to stir his coffee with my finger and then put it in his ear. I wave back. Danny — *Daniel,* excuse me — and I talk for a while, about Ed, about the funeral, about what a wheeler-dealer he was. Then Danny takes out a file marked, "BANK."

"Virginia, did Ed ever ask you to sign anything over the

last year? Any papers? Documents? Agreements?" *(She touches her neck.)*

I can feel it as Danny Spahr asks that question ... the heat begins to rise on my collarbone.

"I was *always* signing *something* or other. Ed was such a one-man band, wheeling and dealing" ....

Danny's staring at me. Ed always said I couldn't keep my mouth shut. I told Tootie about the papers when I visited her and her new husband in Boca Raton last April. I tell Tootie everything, could she have told—?

"Virginia, did you sign anything that looked official?"

He delivered our milk. You can't lie to a blue-eyed boy who used to deliver your milk. I nod. He hands me the papers from the file. Business loans from Bob O'Klock's bank to "Ed Carpolotti, Inc." Secured with equipment, machinery, high-boys, low-boys, tractors, bulldozers. Every asset of the company. Business loans — signed *personally.* Which means — since Ed got me to sign the papers — that I am now personally responsible for these loans — totalling over a half million dollars. Danny tells me Ed was behind in payments. Six months behind. The bank has frozen my assets. The CDs, the IRAs, the savings and checking accounts. Frozen, explains Danny, is a euphemism. They're going to *take* the money. Unless I can find a way to pay off the loan ... within the week. On the way out of the building, I see Bob O'Klock through the glass doors again. His gray suit, his pinstripe hair. What I do next I have not done before in my life. I hurry out of his bank so he will not see me. I turn my head. I run away. *(Pause.)*

I go home to the house on Bray Barton. Still lots of flowers and food leftover from the funeral. In the refrigerator there's a casserole made up entirely of boiled apples, Spam, and noodles. Nobody knows who brought it. It's pretty scary, but Debbie said we should keep it until it learns to talk. I go into Ed's den where he spent most of his time ... at night on the phone — talking to his foremen, Joy. Other men. Sometimes he'd shut the door. I go into the sun room ... where *I* live. There are three messages waiting for me on the answering machine Debbie bought us to prove she really phones home on Sundays. The first is from Tootie in Boca Raton, telling me George Erskine died at his office at the glass factory. Keeled over in the middle of a meeting with his auditor. He and Nancy were to go to Hilton Head on Saturday. The second is from Debbie, telling me she's been invited to a writer's conference in Saskatchewan. For some reason she has to pay for it herself — she even mentions the exact amount — and would I like to get away from town and babysit the twins for a week? The third is from a voice I don't know well.

"Gin, hey, this is Dino DiSperbio, like ta' talk to ya', like ta' take ya' ta' lunch, gimme a call. *(Beat.)* I hate these fuckin' things." *(She looks out.)*

Well, that's what he *said*. I find his number in Ed's book, call him back.

"Mr. DiSperbio, I'd love to go to lunch, but to tell you the truth, I'm just not basically up to it yet." There's a pause.

"Well, we have some business to discuss, Gin."

"Well, I'm free now, Mr. D —"

"Hey, not over the phone."

I agree to meet him the next day at The Green Mill Luncheonette. Everybody in town likes to do business at the Green Mill Luncheonette instead of in their offices. I don't know what they do in their offices. Eat lunch, I guess. When I go in, Dino DiSperbio is waiting for me at a booth in the back. I won't say Mr. DiSperbio is fat ... but almost anyone else would.

"Siddown, Gin." (I do.) "Gin, ya' look good. Are you wearing any federal wiretapping equipment?"

This is the first time I have ever been asked this question, but I think I handle it well.

"Uhhh ... *no.* No, I'm not. Not today anyway. Thank you."

"Gin, I'll get to the point. Ya' know, your husband, Ed, he was a real wheeler-dealer. We had a lotta fun together. Lotta laughs. Lotta cups a' coffee."

He cuts into a piece of peach pie.

"Ed ever ask you to sign any papers?"

My collarbone has been on fire since I heard his voice on the phone the night before.

"See, Ed, he wanted to sell me half of this landfill he owned. I think he needed the money, Gin, and I told him, I said, 'Hey, Ed, I don' think I wanna buy into a partnership, but I tell ya' what: I'll *loan* you some money at a good percentage. How much ya' need? And Ed told me. And I give it to 'im."

"How much did you give him?" I ask.

"Half a million."

"At what percentage?"

"50."

I am not a financier, but even I know this is not a good rate.

"Do you remember signing a piece a' paper, Gin?"

I nod my head.

"Do you *have* the money, Gin?"

I shake my head.

"Well … whadda we gonna *do?*" *(Beat.)*

Dino is the owner of Smith Trucking. They own no trucks and there has never been a Mr. Smith. I go home to the house on Bray Barton. I look at the answering machine — the red light that says I have four messages. The first is from Tootie in Boca Raton saying Art Wise was found dead in the drug store he owned. The store has been closed by the police. His files have been sealed. The second is from Danny. He has to get back to Bob O'Klock. The third is from Bob O'Klock. Would I like to have lunch at the Green Mill? The fourth is from Debbie. She says her Mazda was in an accident. I assume that means *she* was in an accident, but the way she phrases it, it sounds like the Mazda had a night off and got into trouble. The repairs will cost more than the insurance will pay. She even mentions the exact amount. I have to call somebody. Someone in the family who can help. I pick up the phone and dial Ed's brother Frank.

"What's the problem," he says.

"Not over the phone," I say. The next night I meet Frank

up at the club. In the Grill Room, which we all call the Coal Room. Because of the Coal Wall the James family donated in 1959. Debbie says it looks like something Frank Lloyd Wright would have done if he'd spent too much time in Appalachia. *(She looks out, shrugs, rolls her eyes.)*

Who knows?

Frank grins from a table in the back.

"How ya' doin', Virginia?"

"Fine," I say, "and I'm not wearing a wire." It's strange to look at Frank. Seeing the parts of Ed in him. Like he's a dream of Ed that's not quite right. Frank's a "developer." We talk about the property market. About his son Randy's pending marriage to one of the Wickham girls — which pleases Frank and his wife Lorraine no end. Randy is being groomed to run the business and still lives at home. Debbie calls him Boo Radley without the charm. Over the shrimp cocktail, I start my speech. About Danny, about Bob O'Klock, about Dino. Finally, I stop. And then Frank speaks:

"Virginia, you know, Ed was a real wheeler-dealer."

"How much did he borrow?"

"It's three hundred thousand, Virginia."

"At fifty per cent?" I ask.

Frank looks hurt. "I was his brother, Virginia. *(Beat.)* I gave him 18 per cent and truth be told I'm taking a beating."

I explain to Frank I have no cash, no savings, nothing that's not frozen or encumbered. Frank's still looking at me.

"You have the *house*."

I blink at my husband's brother.

"Virginia, Randy's getting married next month, he and Courtney will be back from St. Bart's on the 1st. They were thinking of building on some property I have behind McCauslen Manor, but.... Well, Randy's always loved your house. He likes old houses, you know. Big old white houses with lots of character. Character's very important to Randy."

He should get one, then, I think.

"And those trees. The big oaks lining the street out front. 'Member how he and Deb used to play together in those trees?"

They *never* played together in those trees. Randy took his pants off and threw rocks at cats from the fourth oak on the right while Debbie stayed in her room reading something called *The Bell Jar*.

"Now, I could arrange to have Rand and Court in there by — well — call it the 15th. New paint, new rugs, Lorraine's got some ideas about the master bedroom...."

I go home to the house on Bray Barton. I look at the answering machine — the red light that says I have six messages. The first is from Tootie saying that George Erskine died when it turned out he was embezzling from the glass factory and that Art Wise was a suicide because of some phony prescription drug deal at the store.

"What's *with* these guys?"

she says, and hangs up. The second is from Danny, who says we have to have a meeting, and he's willing to come to the house. The third is from Bob O'Klock's secretary saying Mr. O'Klock wants to see me, and he's willing to come to the house. The fourth is from Dino, who wants to come by the house with a friend named Vinnie. The fifth is Lorraine, who knows of an apartment for rent behind the shopping mall parking lot. The sixth is from Joy at the office. Do I have any ideas on how to make this week's payroll? *(Pause.)*

I start upstairs to bed. As I go through the hall towards the steps, I stop. Under the front door something sticks out. It's a manila envelope, shoved halfway through. I open the door. It's below zero out. Snow on the lawn, ice on the oaks, the street quiet. I take the envelope and close the door. It's blank. I go upstairs to my bedroom, into my bathroom, lock the door. Ed's hairpieces watch me as I open the manila envelope. It's a white piece of paper with letters pasted on it — like a kidnapper's ransom.

"I HAVE A LIST OF THIRTEEN THINGS ABOUT ED CARPOLOTTI. EMBARRASSING TO HIM AND TO OTHERS. HAVE ONE MILLION DOLLARS READY BY THIS FRIDAY. SMALL BILLS. UNMARKED. IN A SUITCASE. OR I WILL RELEASE THE LIST. TELL NO ONE."

Not surprisingly, it is unsigned. *(Pause. During this next section Virginia becomes increasingly angry, hurt, confused, and desperate.)*

"George Erskine was embezzling from his own glass factory."

"Art Wise was selling prescription drugs under the counter."

"Ed Carpolotti was ..."

What will they say about my husband. Will they say thirteen things? More? What is it about these men? Who built their businesses and grew their families and constructed fortresses with their hands and died so frightened and alone? Who could never tell their wives their secrets — their fears? Ed was Catholic, and I am not, and that was a bone many years ago. But I am beginning to understand some things. I am beginning to understand sin. Not the mortal sins or the venial sins. But the sin of failure. The secular sin that knows no organized religion. Who do you go to when you have committed that? Your lawyer? Your banker? Your brother? Your godfather? No one absolves failure. No one lights a candle. You go *mad*. You pray for death and madness. A cow with your mother in a room in Las Vegas. He had run out of ideas, plans, wheeling and dealing. The last place he dreamed of was a land of gamblers in the middle of a desert. I live in my husband's desert now. I owe three times as much money as I thought I had in the world. I am a widow. I am supposed to be drinking gin and tonics on the terrace of a "townhome" in Boca Raton with Tootie Vaughn. I am a widow and we are supposed to buy new cars after our husbands die. I have not told Tootie. I want so *badly* to tell my friend Tootie. I lay out my silver, my china, my crystal, my jewelry, *everything* I have on the dining room table. I don't know where I can sell it all quickly, but .... It won't come close to what I need. Not for Bob O'Klock or Dino or Frank ....or whoever has sent me this note. *This note.* Friday is two days away. *There are 46 messages on the answering machine,* I do *not* return the calls! *(She begins to hold herself and rock back and forth.)*

I have not told a soul, I have not told a soul, I am screaming so slowly, so dimly, so no one can hear. *Where did I meet
my husband?* *Why can't I remember when and where I met my hus-*
band? *(She shuts her eyes, stops rocking, and makes a decision.)*

I pick up the phone and dial Tootie Vaughn in Boca
Raton! We trade bits and pieces for a while. Who's sick, who's
dead, why Tootie in Boca Raton always seems to know more
about what's going on back at home than anyone who actually lives here. Then I ask her my question. *(Long pause.)*

She says she hasn't a clue where I met Ed. Then I fall
apart and I tell her everything. *(Silence, then she tries to brighten
and picks up her cane.)*

Did you notice this cane? It belonged to my Aunt Stella.
I took care of Stella her last few years — about the time Ed
bought our house and Debbie was teething. Stella was a crazy,
old drunk who had one eye, smoked cigars and drank gin
from a bucket. In pictures she looks like an ancient female
pirate in a wheelchair; wild white hair, a toothless grin behind
her black eyepatch. Debbie says she looked like the illegitimate
daughter of Miss Havisham and the Hathaway shirt man. *(She
looks out.)*

I think I actually *get* that one.

Stella gave me her cane in the nursing home, the day they
took her in. I said,

"Stella, now you hold on to this, you may need it."

She shook her head and winked her eye at me.

"Keep it in a safe place for later. *You'll* need it." *(She looks
at the cane, admires it.)*

I like this. I won't sell this.

It's amazing how the deadlines come on the same day. The bank's deadline. Smith Trucking. Frank. The note. I am sitting in my sun room at 8:30 A.M., waiting for the hordes to descend upon my door. It helped to tell Tootie about everything, about the list. And she promised not to tell a soul. I am frightened. But I am *ready*. I have my cigarettes and my cane and my answering machine. — Let 'em come! The first call comes at nine A.M.

"Ginnie, Bob O'Klock here. Hi. Say: I understand there's a, gee-whillikers, a kinda, kinda *list* somebody's got about Ed and some of his, his wheeling and dealing and well, well, Gin, I just want you to know that I'm sure that whatever's in that list is just a darned pack of lies and the bank will certainly do anything it can to make sure it isn't an embarrassment to you. Or to *anyone else*. We will. We'll do anything. *I'll* do anything. *Anything. Don't worry about the loan.* Just, just keep it to yourself."

And then he hung up. The next call came at ten forty-two.

"Yo, Gin, Dino here. Hey! This list thing. Whaddaya say we call it even, huh? Square one. Zero-zero. Don't call back. I hate these fuckin' things." The last call came before dinner.

"Virginia, Frank here. Long pause. Randy and Courtney will be living at home for the foreseeable future. Call me if you need. Tootie Vaughn says hello."

Tootie! Tootie's blabbed to everybody. And the idea of that list has scared them off! *What's in that list?* What kind of dealings did Ed have with Bob, with Dino, with Frank, with … whomever? For the rest of Friday, I wait for another demand from the author of the note. But it does not come that Friday. Or the next Friday or the Friday after that. *(Long pause, then briskly.)* Within the month, we begin to dissolve the business, sell off the assets. Since the loans have been *forgiven* and the creditors *quieted,* Danny says I will have some money to invest, retire on, buy a new car. I don't *need* a new car. At the office, Joy handles most of the real work. I just sign the papers. The last one I sign I tell Joy:

"I'm recognizing Cuba."

Joy doesn't know what the hell I'm talking about. I'm flying to Wisconsin tonight to babysit the twins, but first I had to come here to the funeral home. Another service. Somebody dies every day. Joy offered to drive me. We're a little early, and she insists on coming inside to wait with me in the smoking lounge. I say I have my cane and a copy of *The Bell Jar,* so I'm fine, but she says she wants to keep me company, and she seems odd, so I don't say no. We've never been close. Joy loved my husband, and that has always made it strange. So we sit in silence. Finally the last viewing begins. I stand up … and Joy is holding a manila envelope, just like the one that was slipped under my door.

"It's from Mr. Carpolotti," she says.

Then she walks away — quickly. I wait until Margaret-Mary Walsh and the rest of the mourners have gone into the parlor. Inside is a list. *(She opens the envelope, takes out a white piece of paper.)*

1) I have never loved any other woman but you.

2) I cannot look at your hand without wanting to hold it.

3) I wanted to build you a house but you loved the one on Bray Barton so much the day we drove by, I never had the chance to change your mind.

4) In my wallet, I keep a picture of you when you were ten years old; I fall in love with you again every time I see it.

5) I think about you every night before I go to bed so I can dream of you in my sleep.

6) *My Friend Irma Goes West* was the best movie I never saw.

7) I have always understood our child more than she could ever imagine.

8) We met at the Green Mill Luncheonette on February 22, 1955.

9) I am writing this in St. Joseph's Hospital. I am less scared than tired.

10) I have made mistakes.

11) *But I think this last plan will work.* Joy has my instructions.

12) You could never keep your mouth shut. I *knew* you would tell Tootie Vaughn about the list and she would tell the world.

13) Mary had a little lamb.

(She lights her cigarette. The lights fade.)

END OF PLAY

PROPERTY LIST

TELL-TALE
  Pacemaker (EMIL)

THE THIEF OF TEARS
  Rings (MAC)

THIRTEEN THINGS ABOUT ED CARPOLATTI
  Gold-headed cane (VIRGINIA)
  Purse (VIRGINIA)
  Cigarette (VIRGINIA)
  Cigarette lighter (VIRGINIA)
  Small manila envelope with white
      piece of paper (VIRGINIA)

COSTUME PLOT

EMIL

> White T-shirt
> Grey socks
> White shirt
> Grey jacket
> Grey pants
> Black belt
> Striped tie
> Handkerchief
> Black shoes
> Gold watch

MAC

> Black leather jacket
> Black velvet and chiffon scarf
> Black blouse
> Black skirt
> Opaque tights
> Black shoes
> 6-8 rings
> Earrings

VIRGINIA

> Navy print dress with belt
> Black jacket
> Pantyhose
> Black-heeled shoes
> Diamond necklace
> Gold watch
> Gold earrings
> Wedding band with diamond band
> Dinner ring

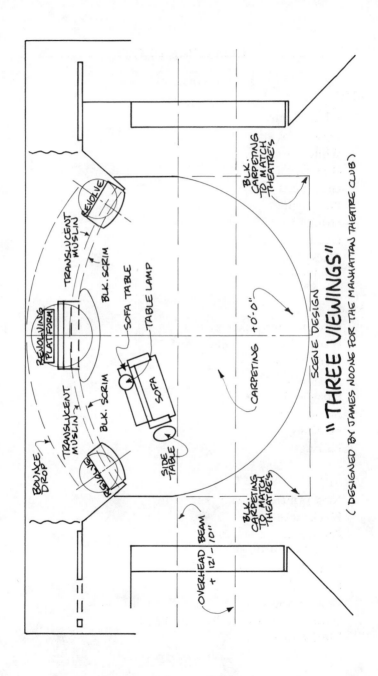

"THREE VIEWINGS"

(DESIGNED BY JAMES NOONE FOR THE MANHATTAN THEATRE CLUB)

SCENE DESIGN

BODACE DROP

TRANSLUCENT MUSLIN

BLK. SCRIM

REVOLVE

REVOLVING PLATFORM

TRANSLUCENT MUSLIN

BLK. SCRIM

REVOLVE

SOFA TABLE

TABLE LAMP

SIDE TABLE

SOFA

CARPETING ±0'-0"

BLK. CARPETING TO MATCH THEATRE'S

BLK. CARPETING TO MATCH THEATRE'S

OVERHEAD BEAM + 12'-10"

NEW
PLAYS

THE LIGHTS
by Howard Korder

THE TRIUMPH OF LOVE
by James Magruder

LATER LIFE
by A.R. Gurney

THE LOMAN FAMILY PICNIC
by Donald Margulies

A PERFECT GANESH
by Terrence McNally

SPAIN
by Romulus Linney

Write for information as to
availability
DRAMATISTS PLAY SERVICE, Inc.
440 Park Avenue South   New York, N.Y. 10016

NEW
PLAYS

LONELY PLANET
by Steven Dietz

THE AMERICA PLAY
by Suzan-Lori Parks

THE FOURTH WALL
by A.R. Gurney

JULIE JOHNSON
by Wendy Hammond

FOUR DOGS AND A BONE
by John Patrick Shanley

DESDEMONA, A PLAY ABOUT A
HANDKERCHIEF
by Paula Vogel

*Write for information as to
availability*
DRAMATISTS PLAY SERVICE, Inc.
440 Park Avenue South   New York, N.Y. 10016